COLDPLAY
FOR CLASSICAL PIANO

Cover Photo by Andy Paradise/Getty Images

— PIANO LEVEL —
LATE INTERMEDIATE/EARLY ADVANCED

ISBN 978-1-4950-0087-4

HAL•LEONARD®
CORPORATION

7777 W. BLUEMOUND RD. P.O. BOX 13819 MILWAUKEE, WI 53213

Visit Hal Leonard Online at
www.halleonard.com

Visit Phillip at
www.phillipkeveren.com

PREFACE

Since forming in the mid-90s, Coldplay has created a body of work that is loved by fans around the world. The British rock band's musical style has been called "limestone rock," "meditative," and "blue romantic." Whatever moniker is assigned, one thing is for certain – their sound is unique and compelling.

This collection of arrangements explores their songs within the framework of a variety of pianistic styles. The word "classical" is a limiting one. I did not attempt to pair each song with a particular classical era (Baroque, etc.). Instead, the notion was to create a piano piece that feels and sounds like it was designed to be a piano solo from its inception – not simply an arrangement of a popular tune.

Musically yours,

Phillip Keveren

BIOGRAPHY

Phillip Keveren, a multi-talented keyboard artist and composer, has composed original works in a variety of genres from piano solo to symphonic orchestra. Mr. Keveren gives frequent concerts and workshops for teachers and their students in the United States, Canada, Europe, and Asia. Mr. Keveren holds a B.M. in composition from California State University Northridge and a M.M. in composition from the University of Southern California.

CONTENTS

AMSTERDAM

Words and Music by GUY BERRYMAN,
JON BUCKLAND, WILL CHAMPION
and CHRIS MARTIN
Arranged by Phillip Keveren

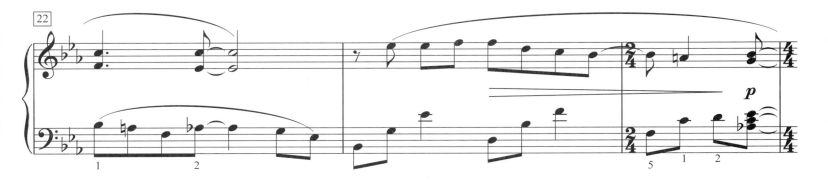

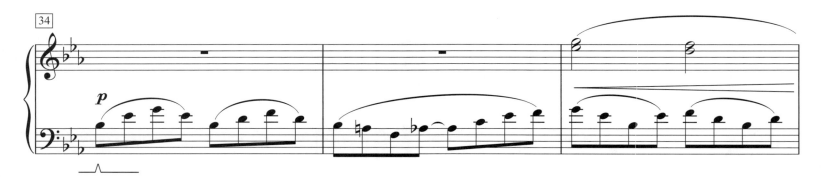

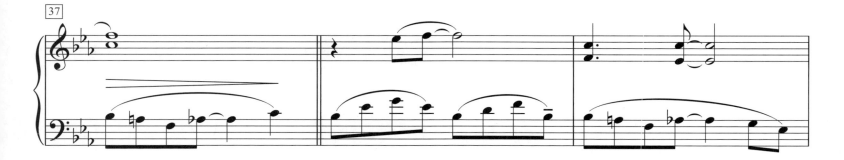

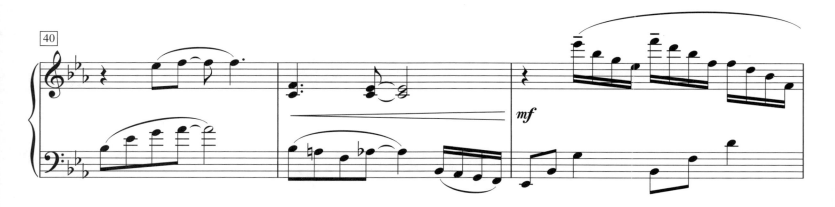

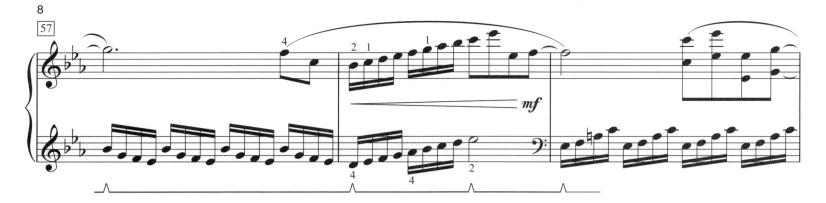

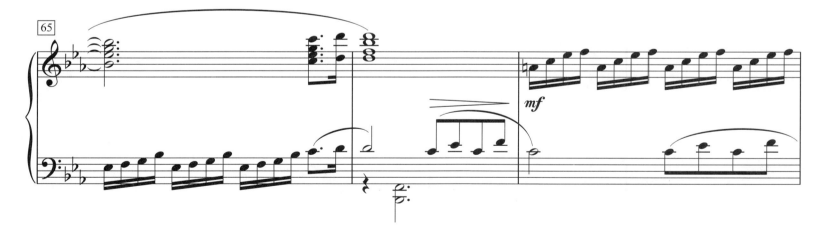

IN MY PLACE

Words and Music by GUY BERRYMAN,
JON BUCKLAND, WILL CHAMPION
and CHRIS MARTIN
Arranged by Phillip Keveren

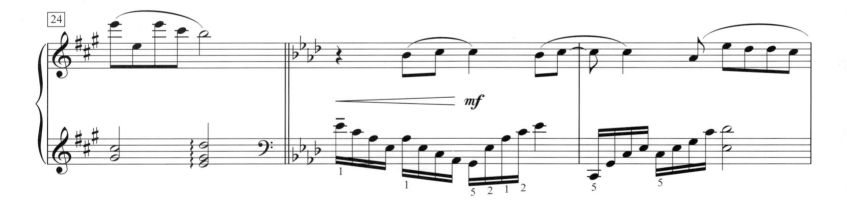

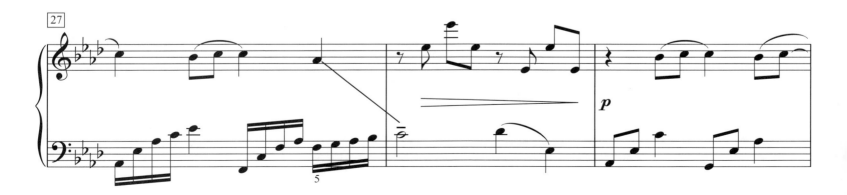

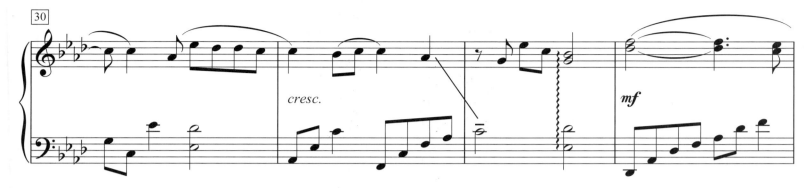

ATLAS
from THE HUNGER GAMES: CATCHING FIRE

Words and Music by GUY BERRYMAN,
JON BUCKLAND, WILL CHAMPION
and CHRIS MARTIN
Arranged by Phillip Keveren

CHRISTMAS LIGHTS

Words and Music by GUY BERRYMAN,
WILL CHAMPION, CHRIS MARTIN
and JONNY BUCKLAND
Arranged by Phillip Keveren

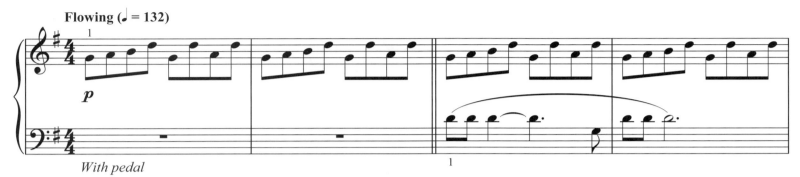

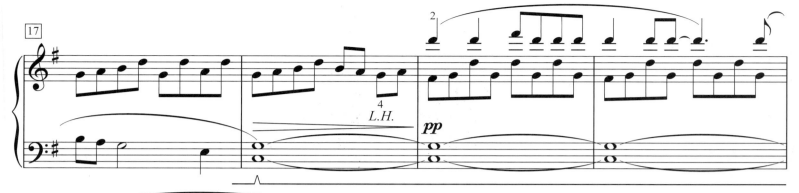

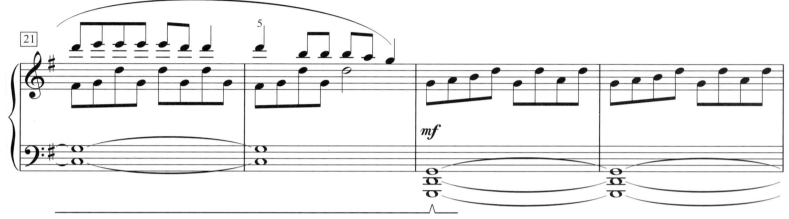

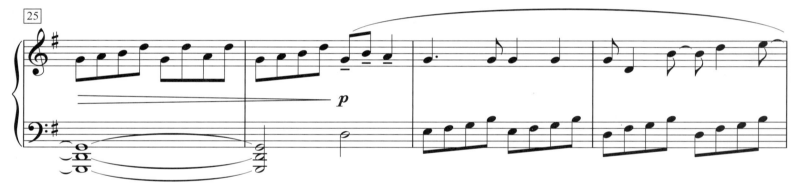

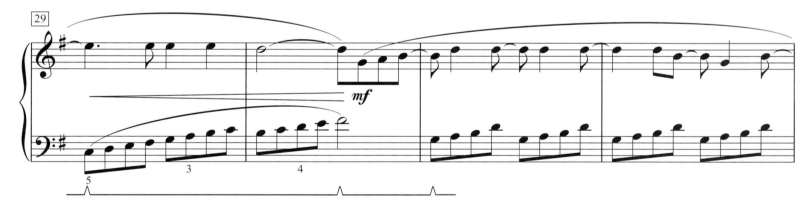

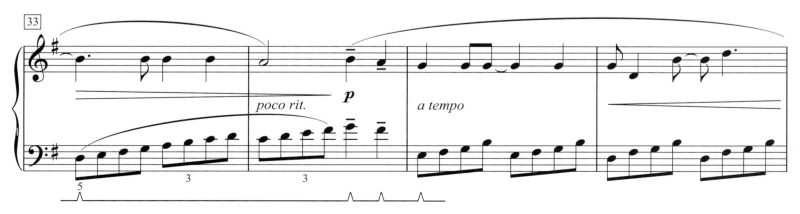

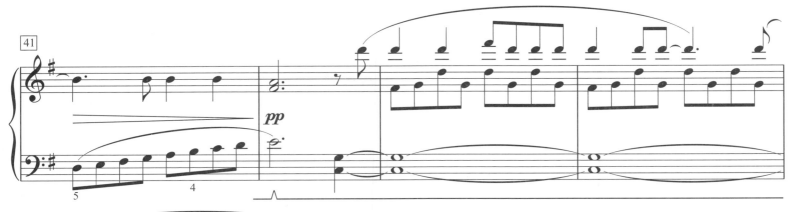

Slower, with a lilt ($\quarternote$ = 126) ($\eighth\eighth$ = $\overset{3}{\triplet{\quarternote\eighth}}$)

CLOCKS

Words and Music by GUY BERRYMAN,
JON BUCKLAND, WILL CHAMPION
and CHRIS MARTIN
Arranged by Phillip Keveren

Relentlessly (♩ = 130)

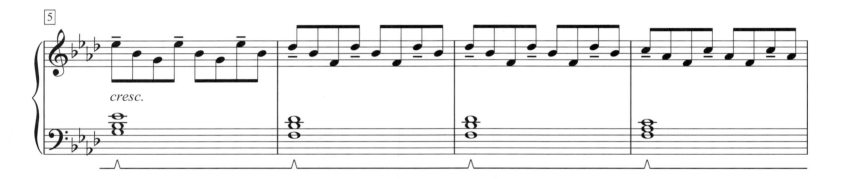

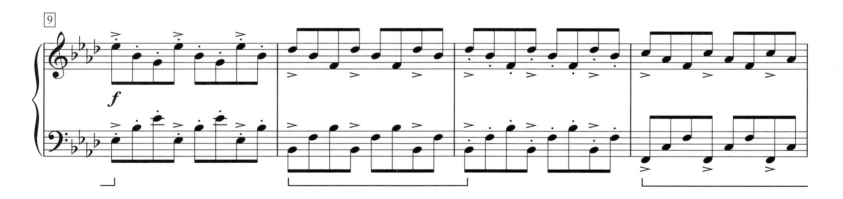

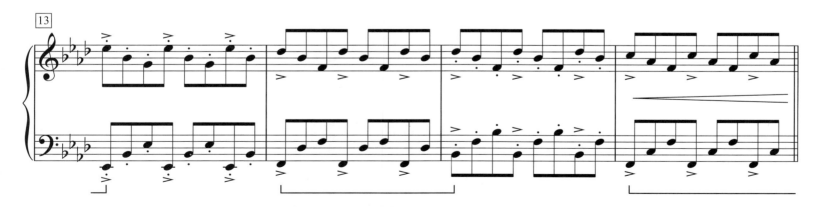

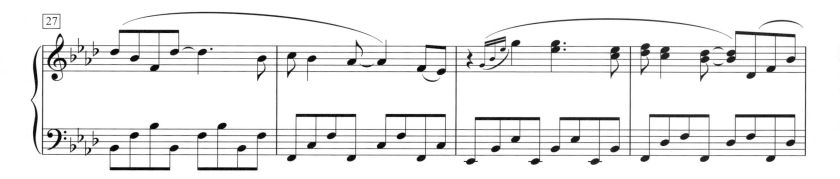

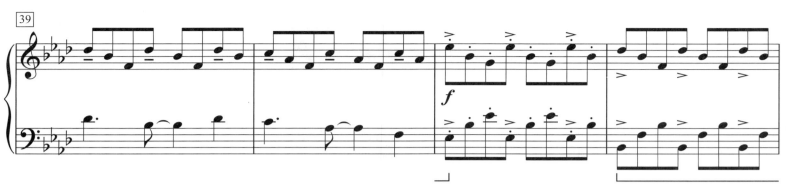

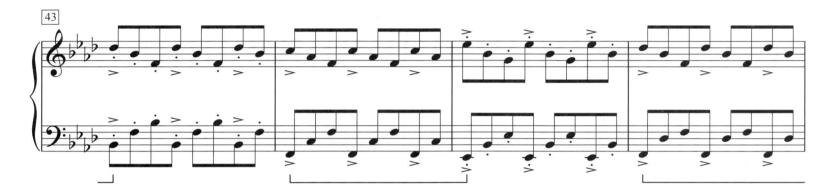

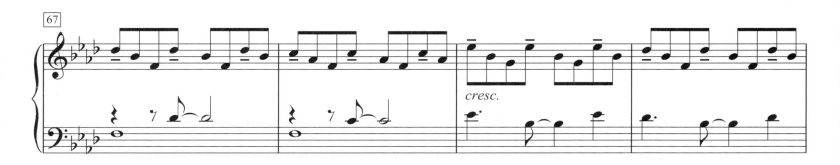

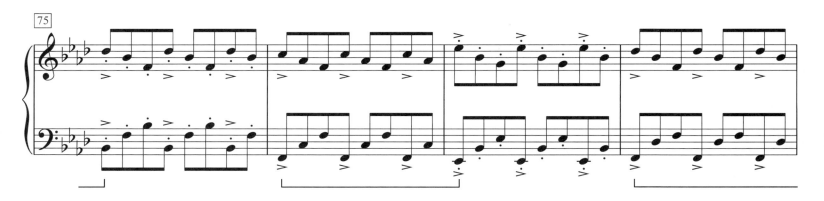

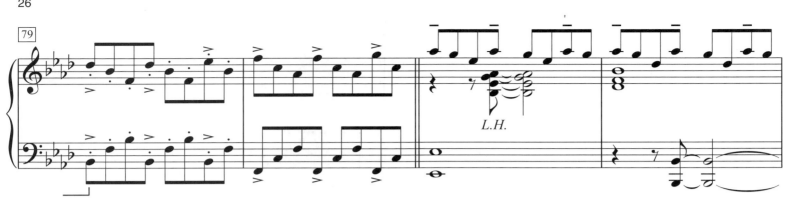

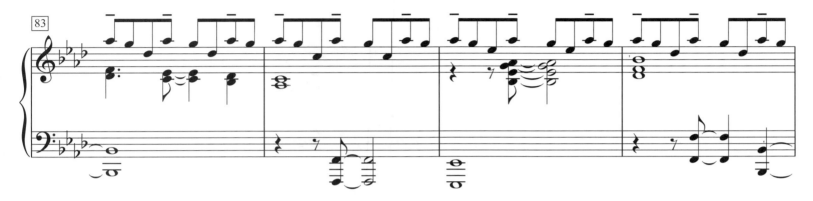

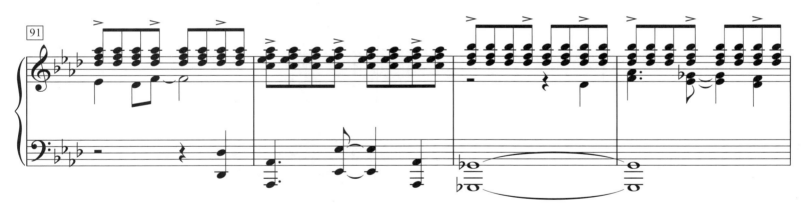

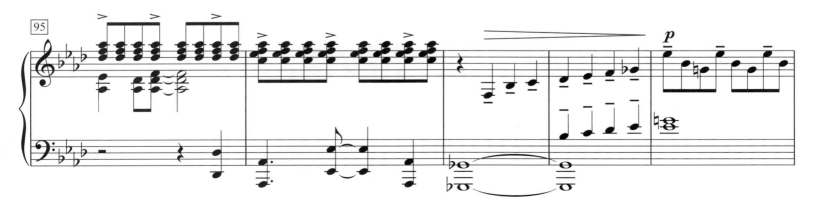

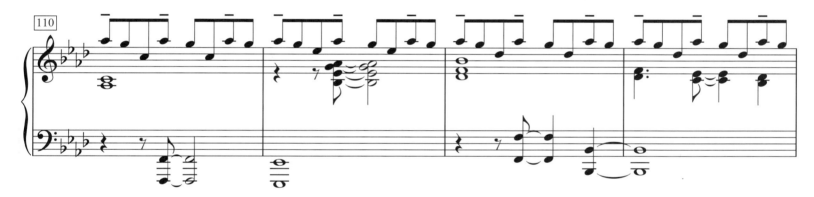

EVERYTHING'S NOT LOST

Words and Music by GUY BERRYMAN,
JON BUCKLAND, WILL CHAMPION
and CHRIS MARTIN
Arranged by Phillip Keveren

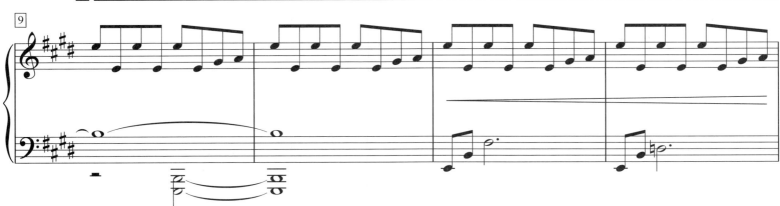

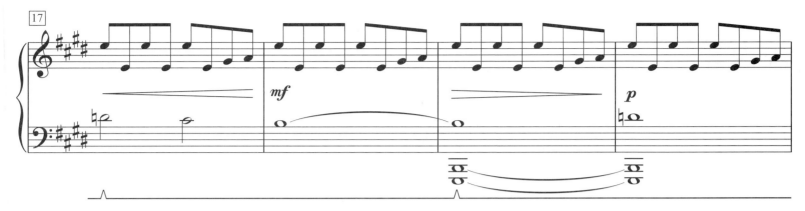

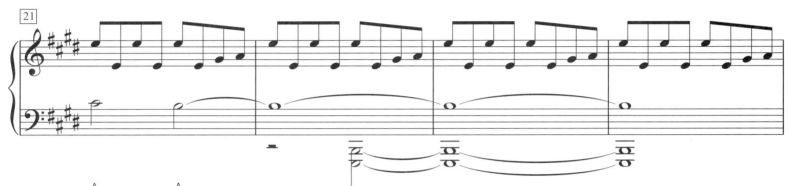

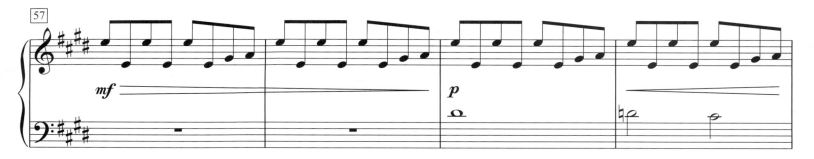

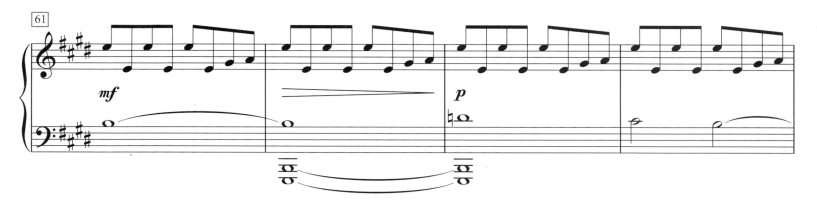

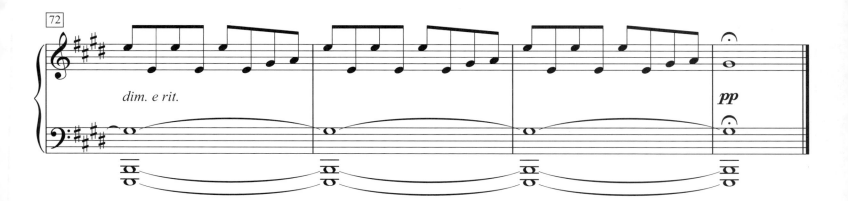

FIX YOU

Words and Music by GUY BERRYMAN,
JON BUCKLAND, WILL CHAMPION
and CHRIS MARTIN
Arranged by Phillip Keveren

With melancholy (♩ = 69)

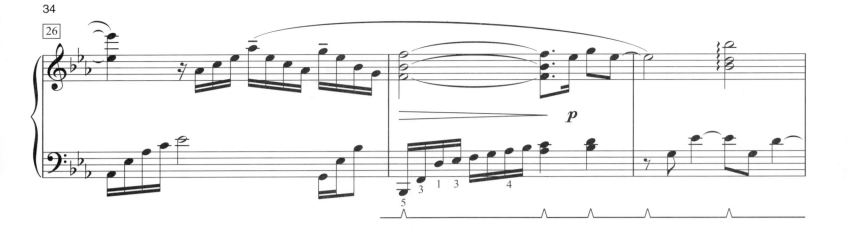

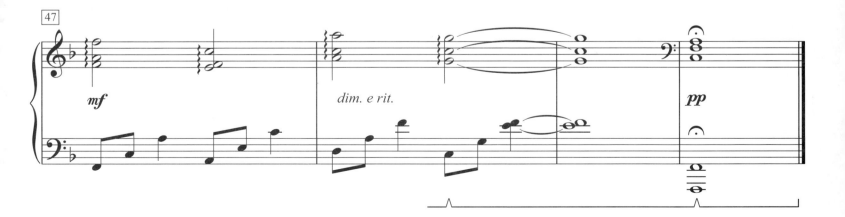

MAGIC

Words and Music by GUY BERRYMAN,
JON BUCKLAND, WILL CHAMPION
and CHRIS MARTIN
Arranged by Phillip Keveren

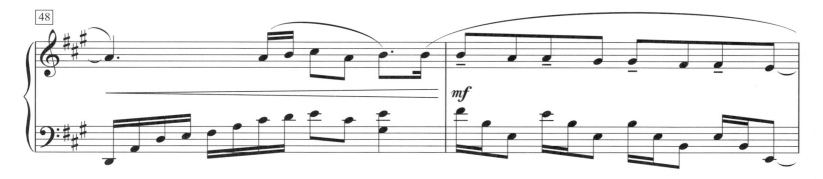

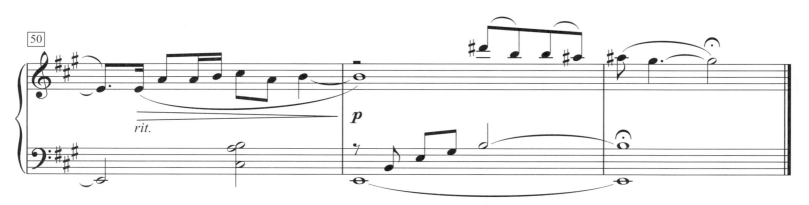

PARADISE

Words and Music by GUY BERRYMAN,
JON BUCKLAND, WILL CHAMPION,
CHRIS MARTIN and BRIAN ENO
Arranged by Phillip Keveren

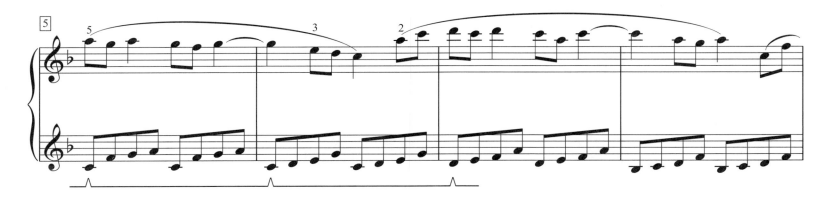

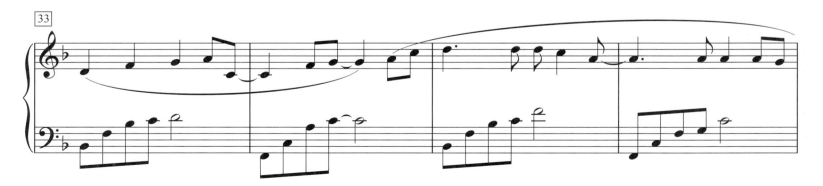

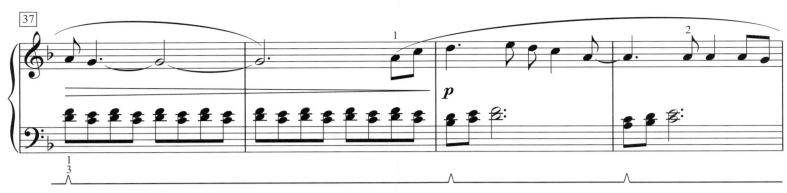

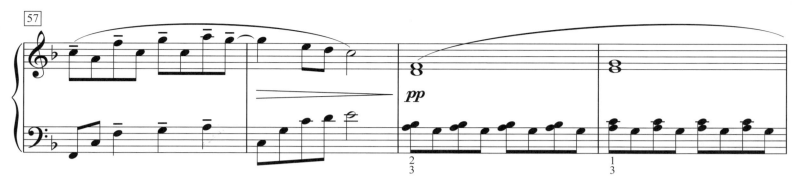

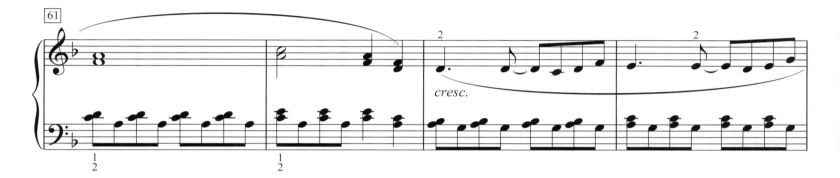

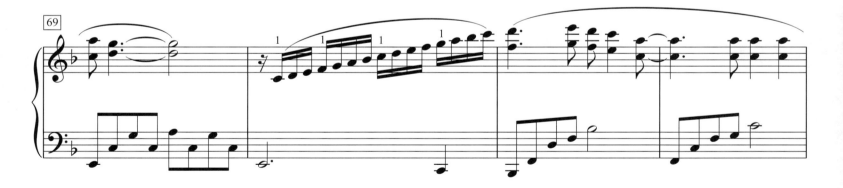

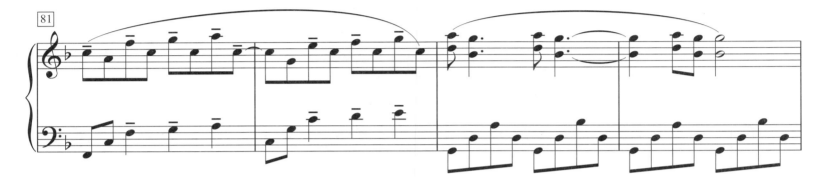

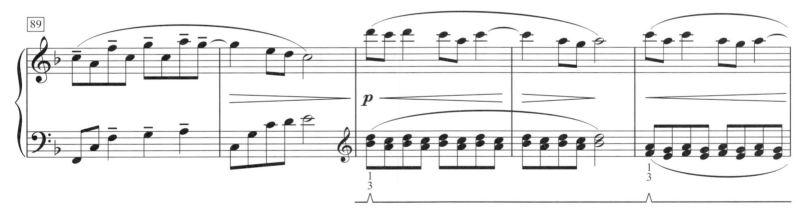

A SKY FULL OF STARS

Words and Music by GUY BERRYMAN,
JON BUCKLAND, WILL CHAMPION,
CHRIS MARTIN and TIM BERGLING
Arranged by Phillip Keveren

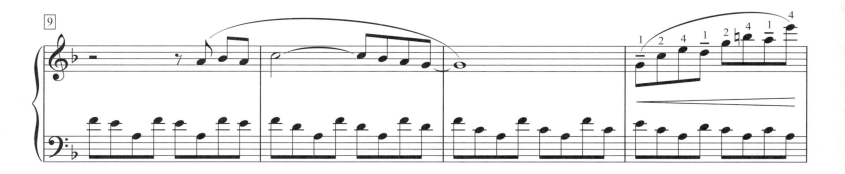

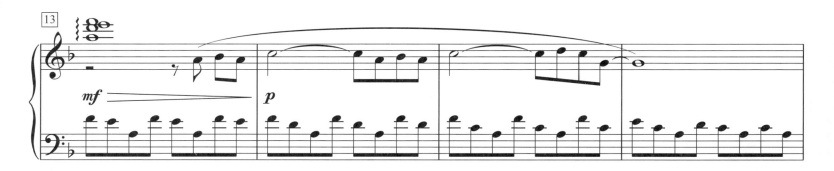

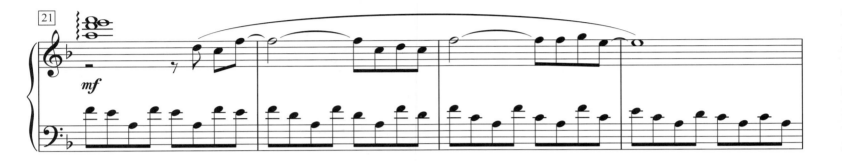

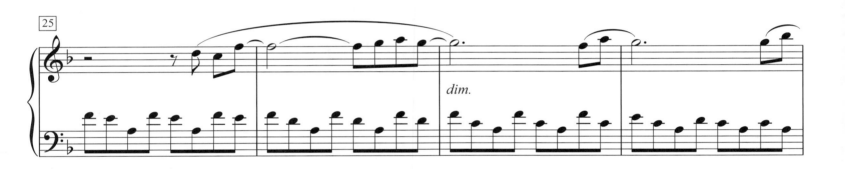

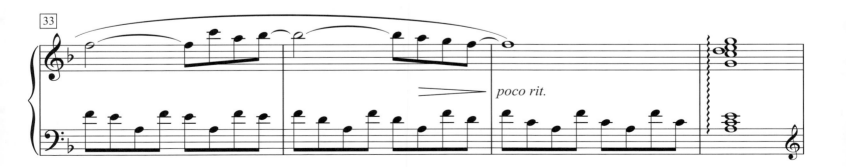

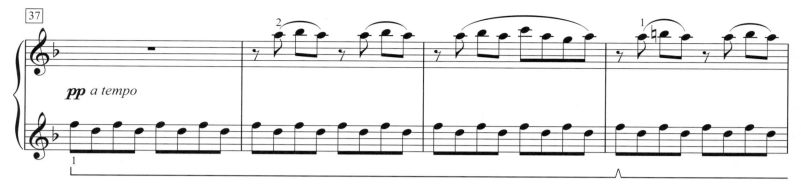

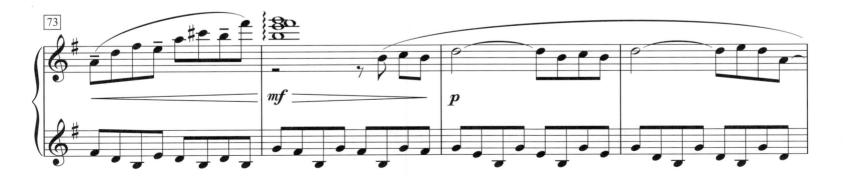

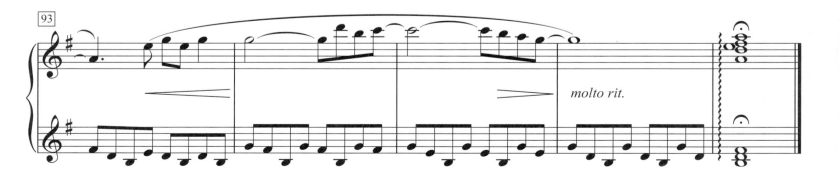

SPEED OF SOUND

Words and Music by GUY BERRYMAN,
JON BUCKLAND, WILL CHAMPION
and CHRIS MARTIN
Arranged by Phillip Keveren

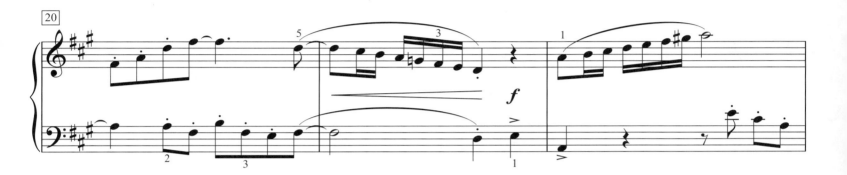

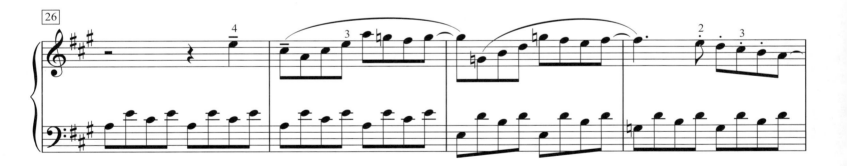

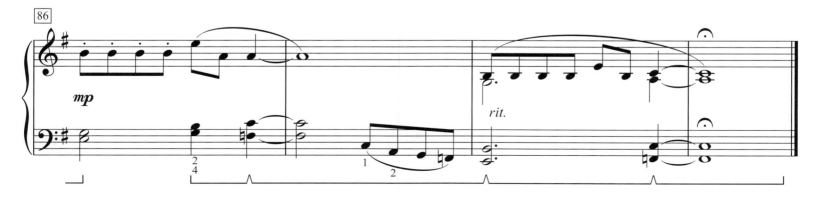

VIVA LA VIDA

Words and Music by GUY BERRYMAN,
JON BUCKLAND, WILL CHAMPION
and CHRIS MARTIN
Arranged by Phillip Keveren

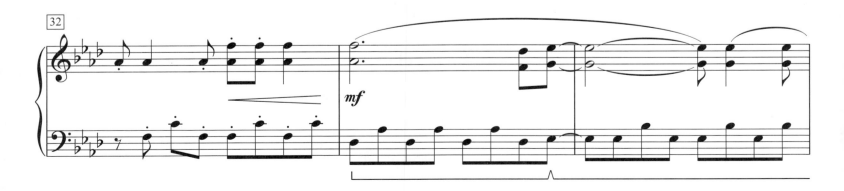

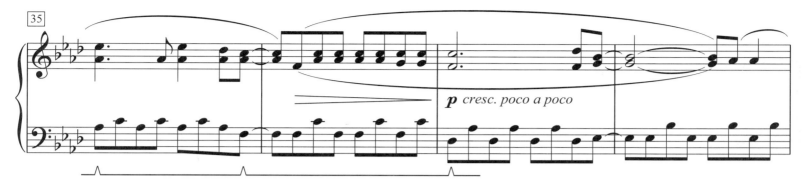

p cresc. poco a poco

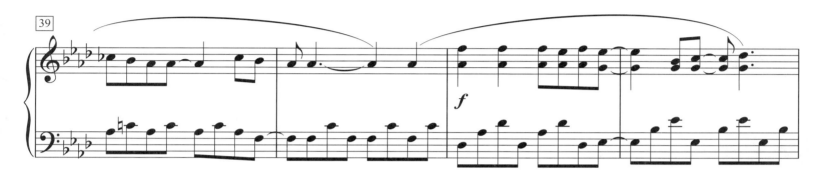

f

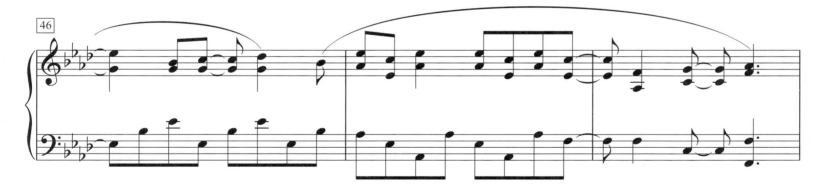

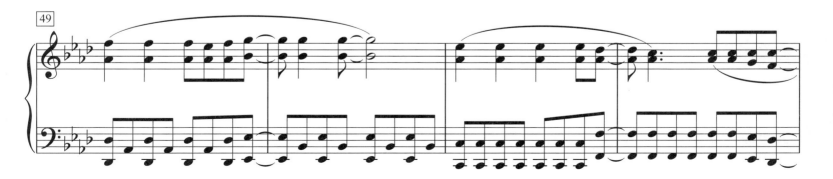

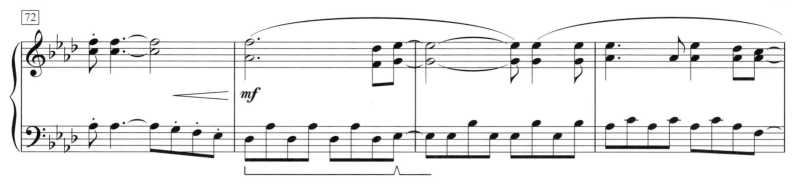

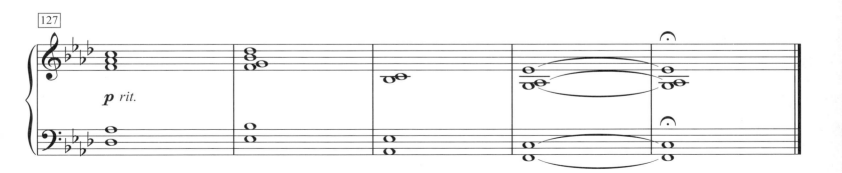

TROUBLE

Words and Music by GUY BERRYMAN,
JON BUCKLAND, WILL CHAMPION
and CHRIS MARTIN
Arranged by Phillip Keveren

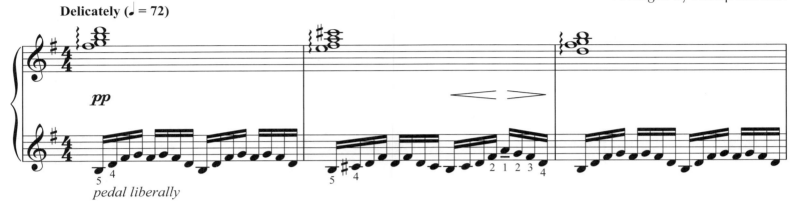

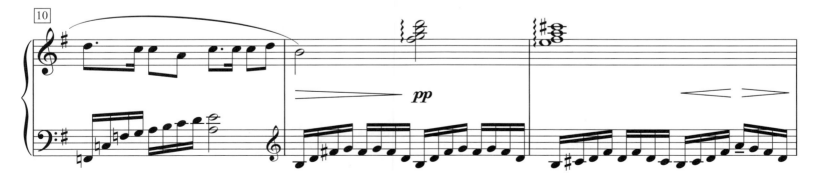

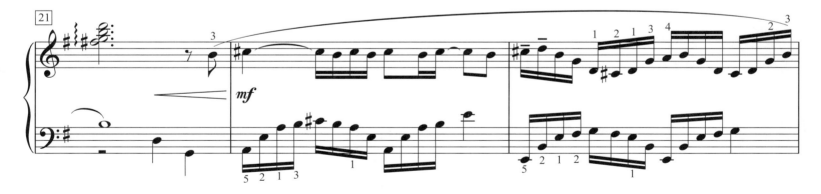

WE NEVER CHANGE

Words and Music by GUY BERRYMAN,
JON BUCKLAND, WILL CHAMPION
and CHRIS MARTIN
Arranged by Phillip Keveren

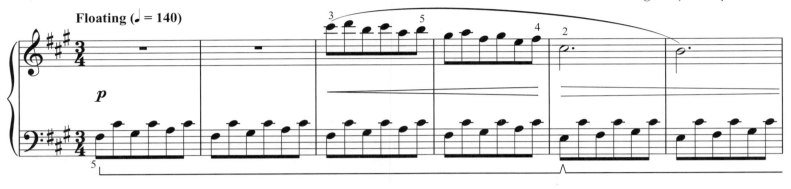

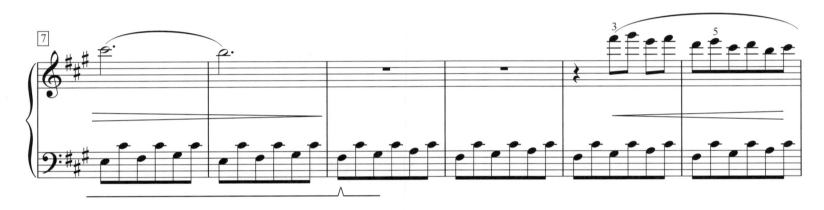

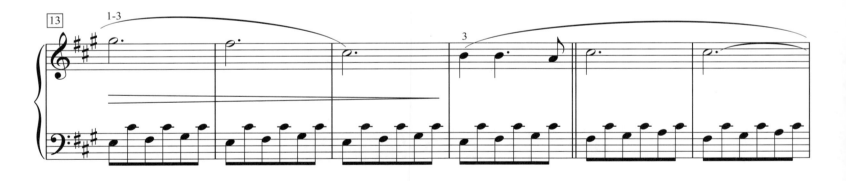

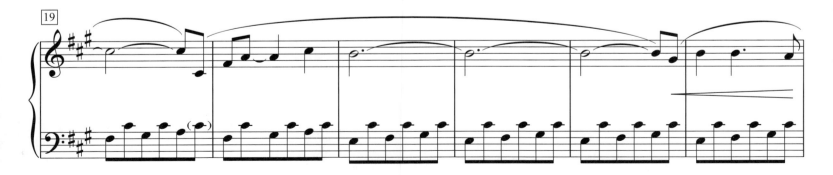

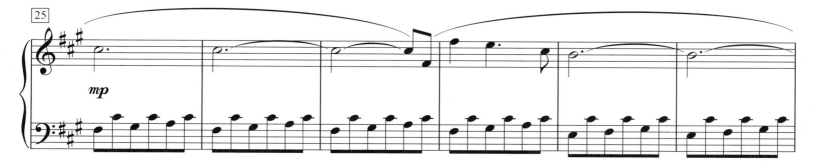

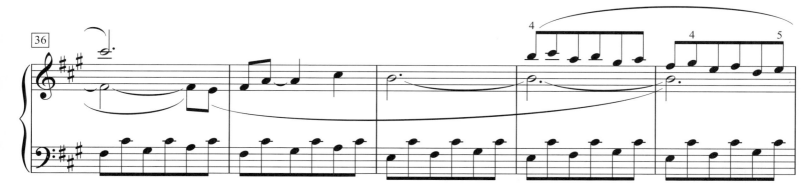

R.H. over L.H.

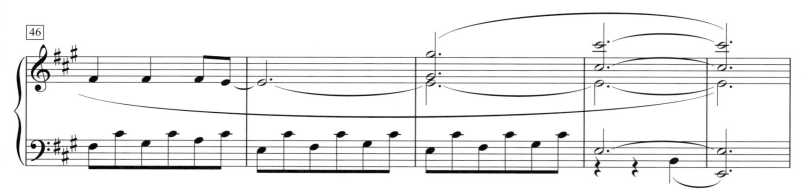

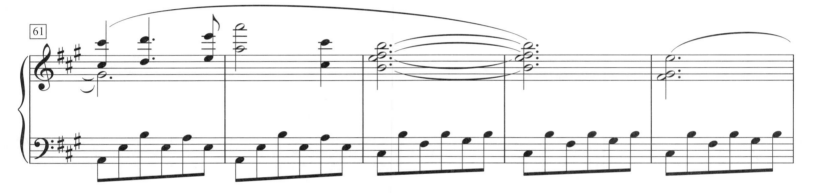

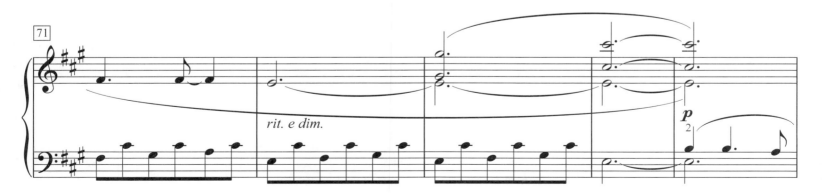

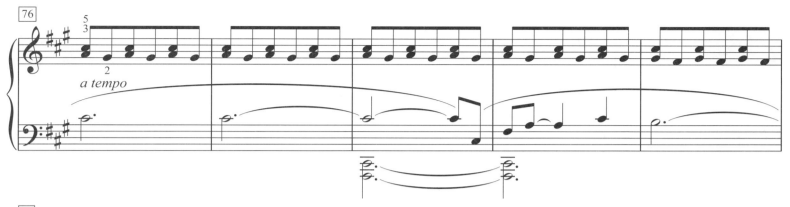

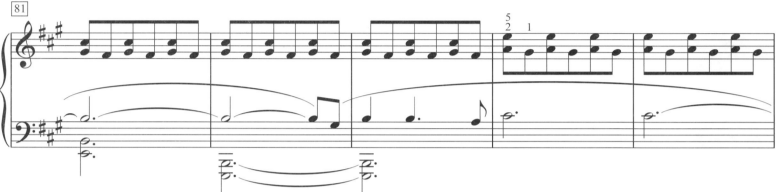

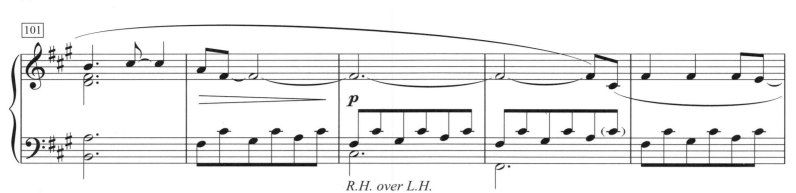

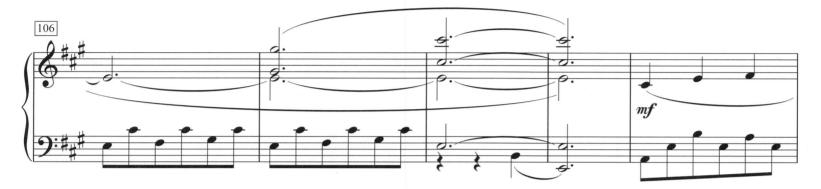

R.H. over L.H.

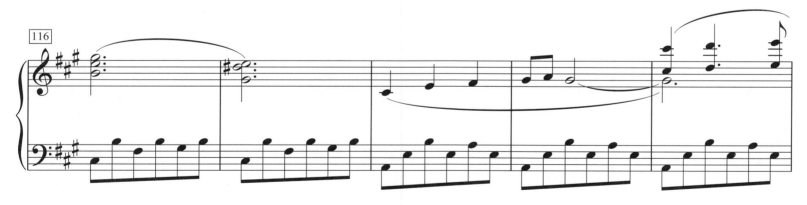

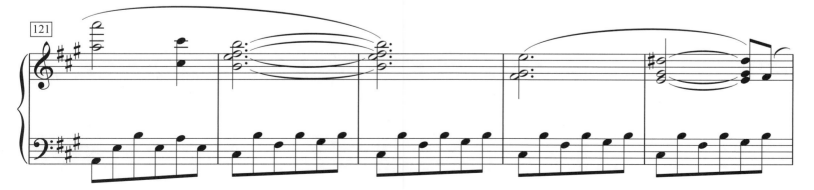

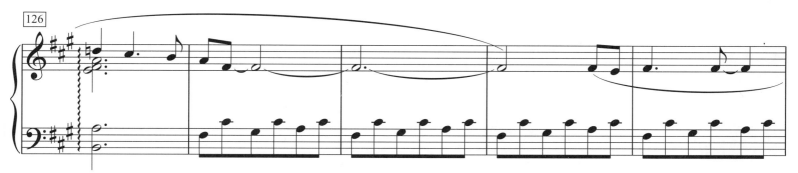

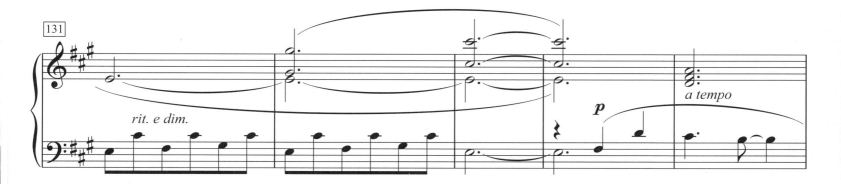

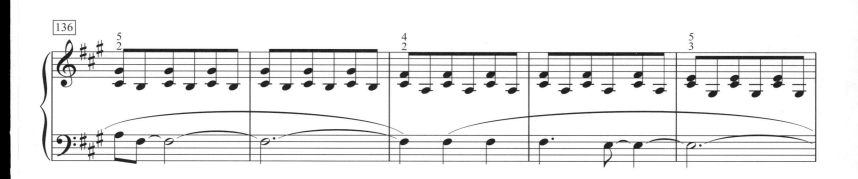

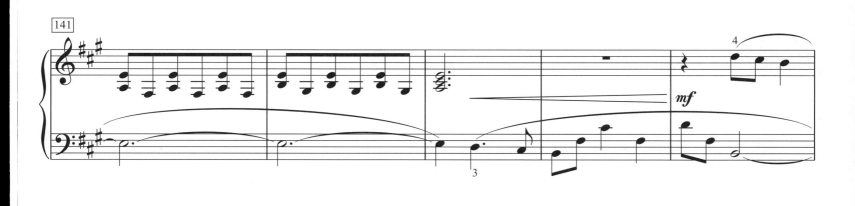

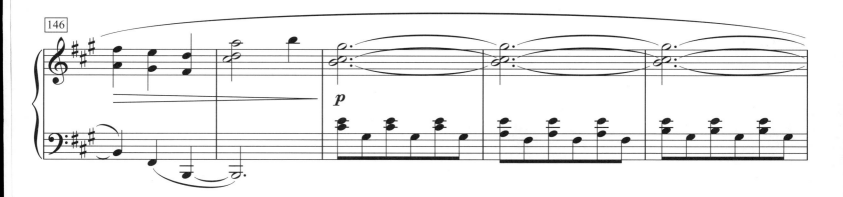

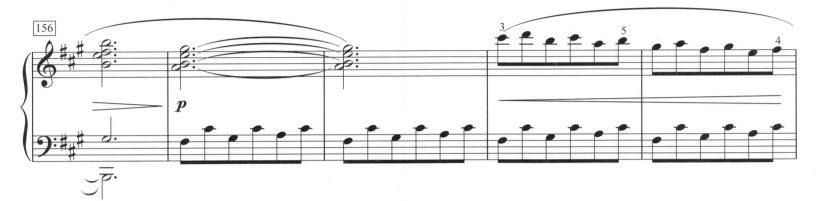

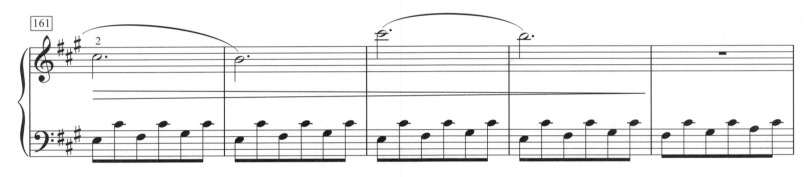

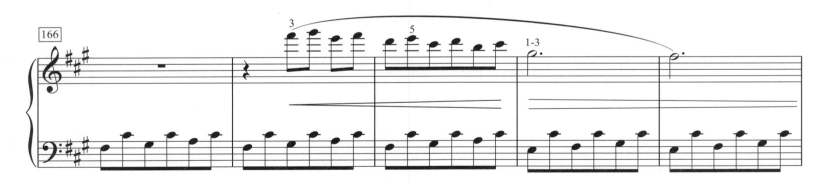

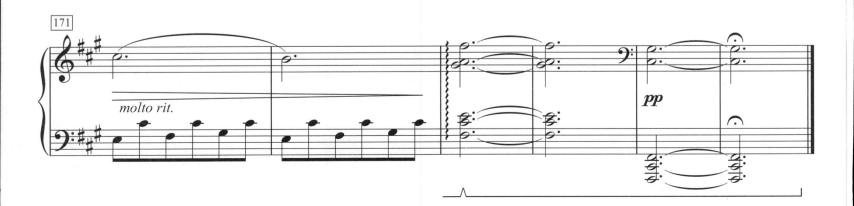